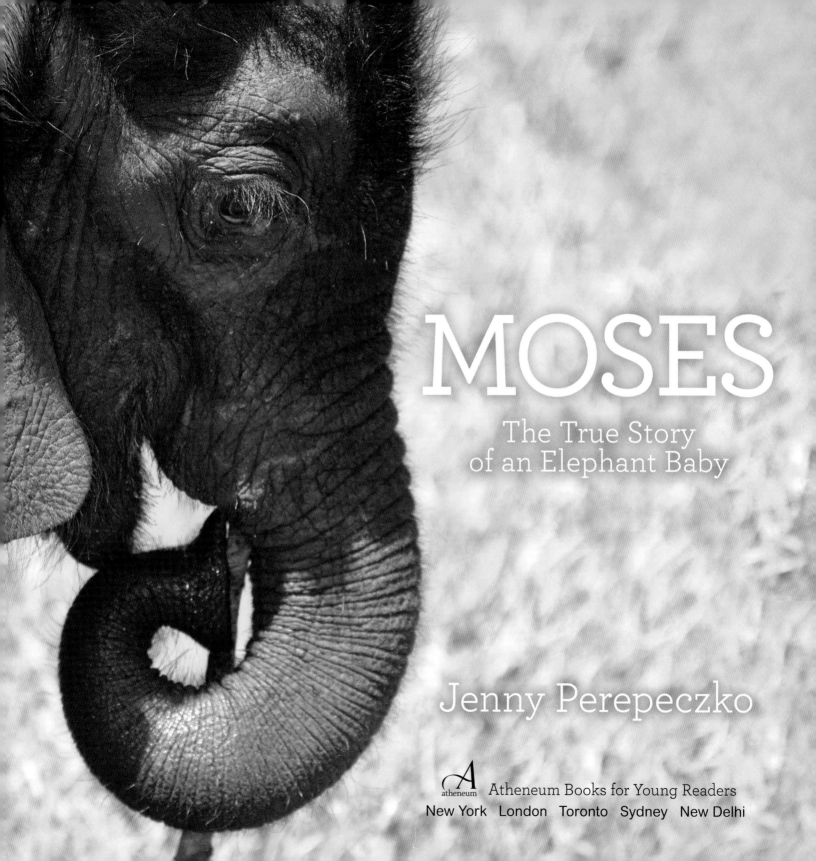

MOSES

The True Story of an Elephant Baby

Jenny Perepeczko

Atheneum Books for Young Readers

New York London Toronto Sydney New Delhi

ATHENEUM BOOKS FOR YOUNG READERS
An imprint of Simon & Schuster Children's Publishing Division
1230 Avenue of the Americas, New York, New York 10020
Copyright © 2014 by Jennifer Anne Perepeczko
The following photographs were reprinted by permission of the rights holders:
Pages 1, 3, 7 (Moses with dog), 8, 9 (eye; mouth), 11, 12 (cat; dog; donkey), 13, 16 (three photos
of Jenny and Moses), 24, 25, 26, 27 (Moses facing little brown dog; Moses facing big brown dog;
Moses with big brown dog), 28, 45 / Mandi Kelsall
Pages 6, 7 (Moses with Jenny and bottle; Moses with Catherine), 10, 17, 19 (three photos of Moses
and coffee cup), 20, 22, 27 (Moses with little brown dog and Jenny; Moses with black dog), 32, 36,
37, 38, 41 / Louise Perepeczko
Pages 7 (Moses with Louise), 18, 34 / Cheryl Perepeczko
Pages 14, 29, 30, 31 / Les Bond
Page 42 / Ben Tutton

For information about special discounts for bulk purchases, please contact Simon & Schuster
Special Sales at 1-866-506-1949 or business@simonandschuster.com.
The Simon & Schuster Speakers Bureau can bring authors to your live event. For more information
or to book an event, contact the Simon & Schuster Speakers Bureau at 1-866-248-3049
or visit our website at www.simonspeakers.com.
Book design by Lauren Rille and Ellice Lee
The text for this book is set in Archer.
Manufactured in China
0614 SCP
First Edition
2 4 6 8 10 9 7 5 3 1
Library of Congress Cataloging-in-Publication Data
Perepeczko, Jenny.
Moses : the true story of an elephant baby / Jenny Perepeczko. — First edition.
pages cm
ISBN 978-1-4424-9603-3 (hardcover)
ISBN 978-1-4424-9604-0 (eBook)
1. Elephants—Infancy—Malawi—Lilongwe—Juvenile literature. 2. Elephants—Malawi—
Lilongwe—Biography—Juvenile literature. 3. Orphaned animals—Malawi—Lilongwe—
Juvenile literature. 4. Perepeczko, Jenny—Juvenile literature. 5. Jumbo Foundation—Juvenile
literature. 6. Wildlife rehabilitation—Malawi—Lilongwe—Juvenile literature. I. Title.
QL737.P98P396 2013
599.6713'92—dc23   2013025985

To Catherine
—J. P.

Introduction

Moses was a little elephant who lived in
Lilongwe, Malawi, in Africa.

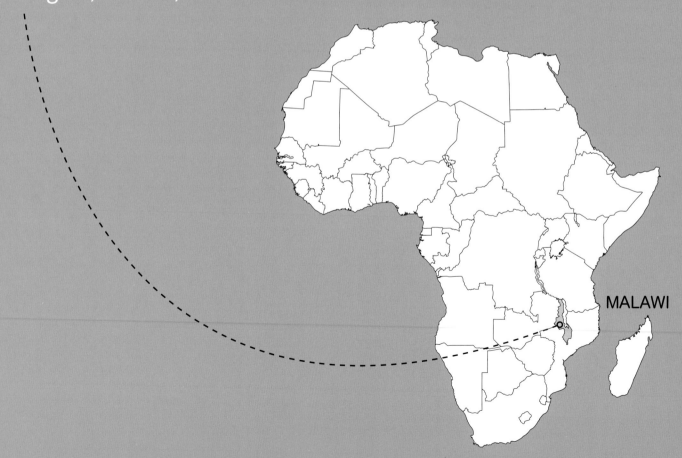

MALAWI

His elephant mama died when he was very little, so he lived at the Jumbo Foundation Elephant Orphanage, where he would stay until he was big enough to go back to his elephant family in the wild.

Moses was found all alone, stuck in a river. His mama had been killed by poachers, and he was running around the bush, looking for somebody to help him—a little elephant cannot look after himself. Perhaps he went to the river because splashing in the water brought back happy memories of playing with his mama. But without her to help him out again, he got stuck. Luckily, some kind rangers rescued him and brought him to the Jumbo Foundation.

The Jumbo Foundation is a place where large, orphaned or injured animals can go to be looked after until they are big enough and well enough to go back to the wild where they belong. These animals need lots of love and special care as they are often hurt and very sad when they arrive, but once they realize that they are loved and safe, they start to heal and become happy again.

○ About 30,000 elephants a year are killed by poachers who want to sell elephant tusks, and the number is getting bigger every year. This means that if poachers are not stopped, there will be no more elephants left in the wild within the next ten years.

It is very important to look after these animals and return them to the wild. The Jumbo Foundation tries to teach people, especially children, about being kind to animals and protecting them. The Jumbo Foundation is six miles outside Lilongwe, Malawi, in Africa, and it is a quiet place with areas of natural bush where the animals can go for walks and feel as if they are still in the wild. The Jumbo Foundation will soon have a big, roomy barn where the animals and their keepers can sleep together at night, because baby elephants can never be left alone. Moses was the first little baby to be rescued by the Jumbo Foundation, and at that time the barn was not yet built, so he spent his nights in the house, sleeping on a mattress on the floor.

JENNY   LOUISE   CATHERINE

At the Jumbo Foundation, Moses lived with his human mama, Jenny; Jenny's grown-up daughter, Louise; Louise's baby daughter, Catherine; and many animal family members too. Moses had lots of adventures with his animal friends, and like all little ones, sometimes he just couldn't help being a bit naughty!

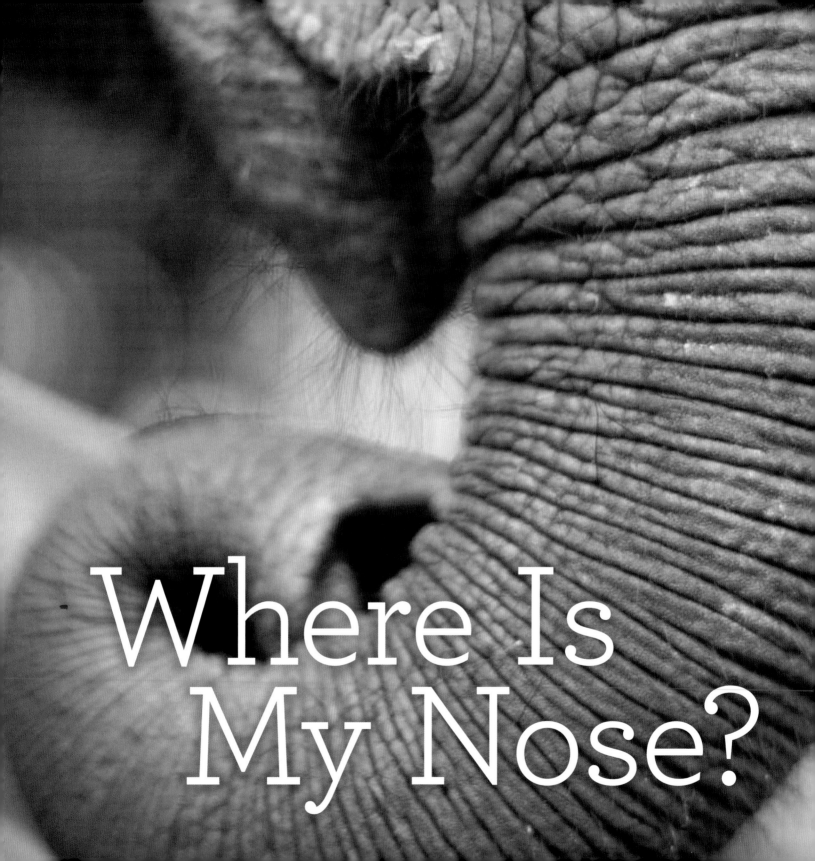

Where Is My Nose?

When Moses woke up in the night, when it was not yet time for his bottle, he thought that Mama should wake up too and play with him. Mama did not think this was a good idea at all, and she tried to lie very still and hope that Moses would just go back to sleep.

One night, when Mama was sleeping, Moses decided to use his trunk to explore her face. He felt her eyes and then put his trunk onto his own eyes and felt them, too. *These feel just like Mama's eyes,* he thought.

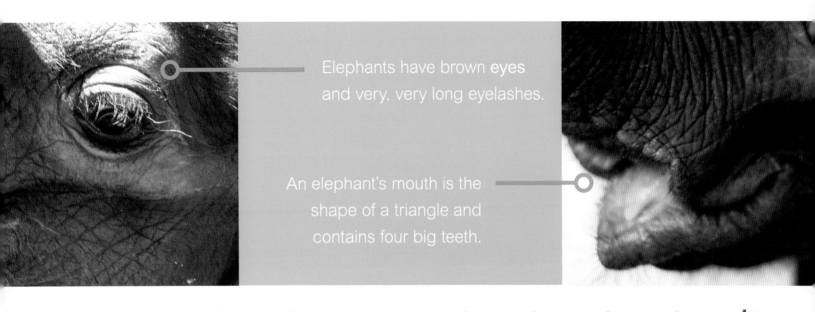

Elephants have brown **eyes** and very, very long eyelashes.

An elephant's mouth is the shape of a triangle and contains four big teeth.

He then put his trunk into Mama's mouth. "Lie down and go to sleep, Moses," said Mama. "It is not good manners to put your trunk into people's mouths, especially when they are sleeping." Moses took his trunk out of Mama's mouth. *Oh dear, she is a bit grumpy,* he thought, *but never mind, I will just feel on my face to see if I have one of those.* And sure enough he felt around until he found his mouth.

Elephant ears are very big with lots of veins. Elephants flap their ears like a fan, which cools the blood in these veins, lowering their body temperature by as much as ten degrees Fahrenheit!

Next, he put his trunk over Mama's ears and felt around inside them.

"Moses, go back to sleep and take your nose out of my ears," said Mama.

Grumpy Mama, he thought. *But what else am I supposed to do if she won't play with me and I really am not tired?* He then felt for his own ears— they were much, much bigger than Mama's, but the inside part felt the same.

Elephants' skin is very thick, up to almost an inch thick in some places, and very wrinkly!

But the outsides felt rather different.

Moses then went back to exploring Mama's face with his trunk and felt her nose. He couldn't remember feeling anything like that on his own face, and he rubbed his trunk over his face again just in case he had missed it before. *Oh no,* he thought, *I don't have one of those.*

Just then Shumba the cat walked up to say hello, and Moses felt over Shumba's face to see if he had a nose. Sure enough, Shumba had one. Moses started to get a bit worried. *Mama has a nose, Shumba has a nose, but I don't....*

He set off to find the other animals to feel if they had noses. Barney the dog had one, and so did his brother, Brandy. Mr. Bo Jangles the donkey had one, and all the other people in the house did too.

Moses felt very sad and went to stand in a corner by himself. *Why am I the only one without a nose?* he thought. Mama came over to make him feel better. "Silly little Moses," she said. "Of course you have a nose, yours is just much bigger than ours. Your trunk is your nose, and you can use it to do all sorts of things. That is what makes you a very special little animal!"

That made Moses very happy. He liked being special, and he was very happy that Mama was awake now and she didn't seem grumpy at all.

A Smelly Time

Like all elephants, Moses used his trunk, which is a very, very long nose, to explore the world. Little elephants are very curious. They use their trunks to find out what something feels like, what it smells like, and to pick things up as well. How useful to do all these things with one part of your body!

With such a long nose, Moses could smell much better than we can. Just imagine how stinky it must be for elephants when there is a terrible odor around!

Moses liked to smell everything he saw, and sometimes that led to trouble. One night after supper, the grown-ups forgot to put away the chili sauce, and nosy little Moses went to find out what was in the dish.

He knew he was not really supposed to take things off the table, but he just couldn't help it—he had to smell what was in that dish. He slowly slid his trunk up the table and into the bowl. . . . Oh dear, that was not a good idea!

Chili burns, especially when it gets into your nose. Moses squealed and ran to his mama, holding up his trunk and rubbing it on her to try and make the sting go away.

Mama gently washed the chili off his little trunk and gave him a cuddle to make him feel better.

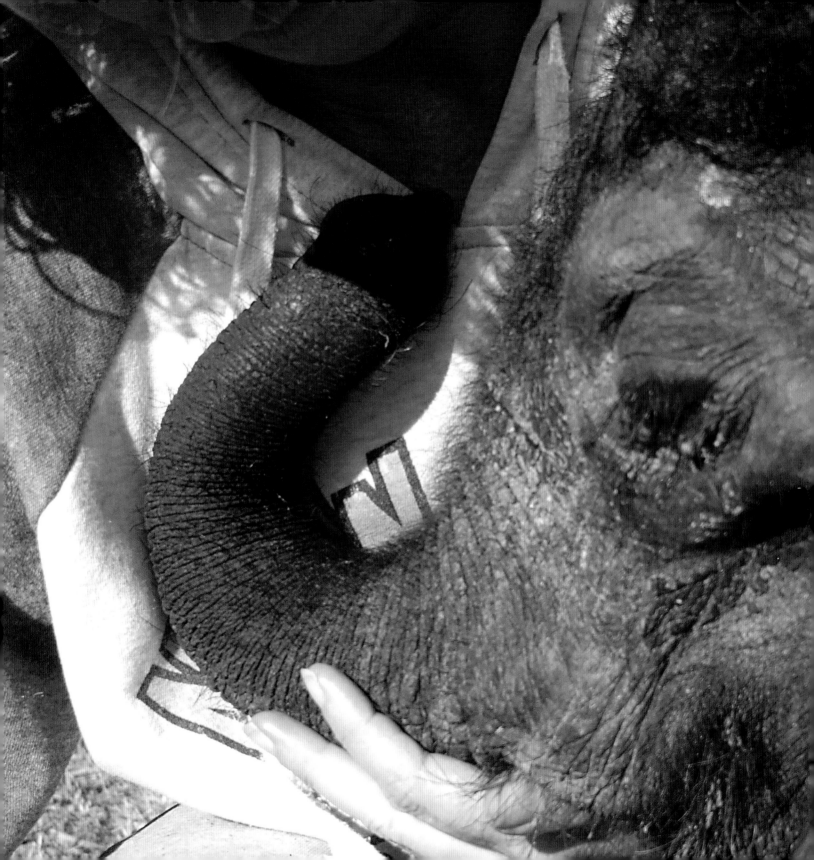

That Nose Gets You Into Trouble, Moses!

Moses liked to pick things up with his trunk and either put them into his mouth or shake them around, a bit like a baby does with a rattle. One day, Moses went into the kitchen on his own. *Goodie,* he thought. *Now I can see what is on all those shelves that Mama won't let me put my nose into.*

Moses put his trunk onto the first shelf and felt around. He could feel something smooth with a nice little handle just big enough for his trunk to fit through—it was a coffee mug. He slid his trunk around the handle and pulled the mug out; it was quite heavy for a little trunk but not too heavy to start shaking around. *This is fun,* thought Moses, and then . . . oops! The mug slipped off his trunk and fell to the floor with a loud crash and smashed into a thousand pieces. Moses got a big fright and ran out of the kitchen as fast as his little legs could carry him!

SLUUURP!

Little elephants love playing with water and their trunks are very useful for splashing. It is just like having a big pool noodle on your face! Moses could move his trunk really fast to make really big splashes. In the wild, elephants like to spray water all over one another. But Moses had dogs, cats, a donkey, and lots of people to splash with water!

One day, when Moses was playing with the water in his paddling pool, he started sucking in with his trunk, and *presto*! It filled up with water just like a giant straw. Moses got a bit of a fright at first and quickly blew his nose hard, and a huge spray of water came out. Moses had discovered a new game! He filled his trunk with water and crept up slowly behind Mama.

Elephants use their trunks like a nose for breathing and smelling, but they can also use it like a straw to suck up water and spray it everywhere. They can also use it for drinking by drawing the water up and squirting it into their mouths.

Elephants can walk very, very quietly. When Moses got close enough, he lifted up his trunk and blew, spraying water all over Mama!

Elephants have a springy cushion underneath their big feet that allows them to walk almost silently, even over dry leaves and twigs.

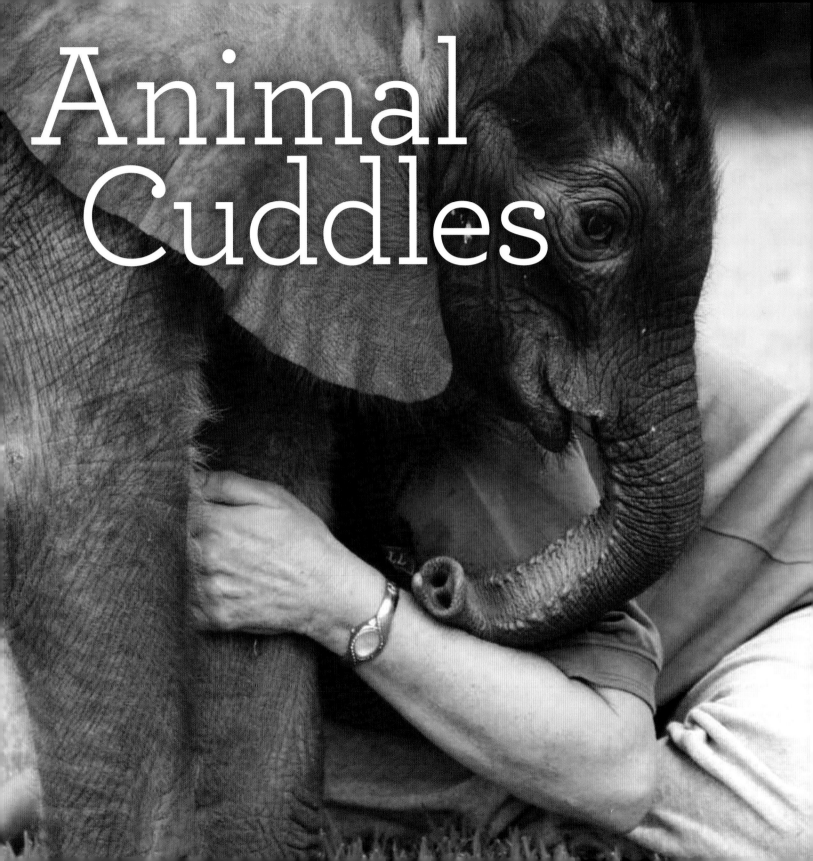

Animal
Cuddles

Elephants love to cuddle with their friends and family. Moses was the baby of the house, and he loved to use his trunk to give everybody big hugs.

Shumba the cat was one of Moses's best friends. He loved to be stroked by Moses's trunk and rubbed himself against Moses's legs to give Moses

a hug back. Shumba often curled up next to Moses at night to go to sleep. *Cats are allowed,* Moses thought, *but not dogs because they are too noisy and bouncy at night.* Sometimes Moses even used his trunk to put Shumba's tail into his mouth, but Shumba didn't mind because he knew that Moses was just a baby and all babies sometimes put funny things into their mouths.

Barney the dog was not quite so sure about this hug. Hey, Moses, your trunk is covering Barney's eyes!

Moses was the boss of all the dogs. He loved playing with them during the day, and they all loved going for walks together, along with the cats and even the donkey.

But Mama said dogs were not allowed inside at night. If the dogs didn't listen and tried to come into the house, then Moses chased them and smacked them with his trunk. But he always greeted them with a big hug in the morning and made friends with them again.

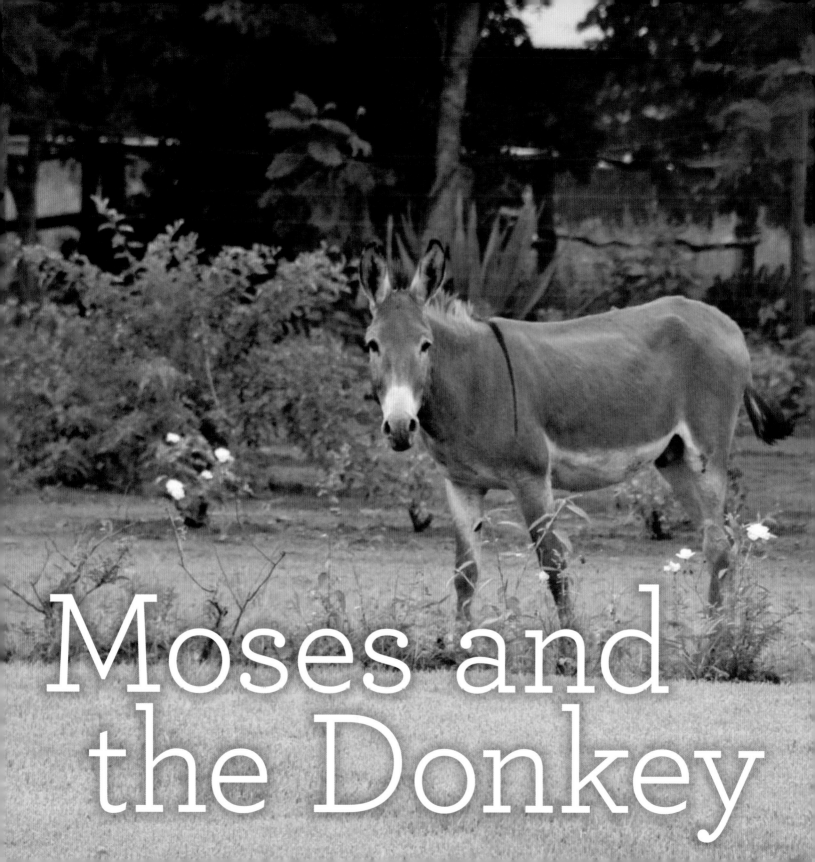

Moses and the Donkey

Mr. Bo Jangles the donkey came to live with the family after he had been rescued by the Society for the Prevention of Cruelty to Animals. Some people had been very mean to him, but at the Jumbo Foundation he grew to be very happy and healthy.

Mr. Bo Jangles loved rolling in the dust and made himself a nice dust bowl every morning. Moses also liked playing in the dust, and he went to play in the dust bowl a few times every day.

Baby elephants learn how to play with dust from watching their mamas, and Jenny had to teach Moses how to do this using her arm and hand as if they were a trunk. Moses watched for quite a long time before he was able to do this for himself, but once he learned how to do it, it became his favorite game. The best place to find good deep dust was in the dust bowl that Mr. Bo Jangles made.

Elephants like to play in the dust and throw it all over themselves. The dust on their skin helps to protect them from sunburn and biting bugs.

But Moses was not always very good about sharing, and when Mr. Bo Jangles came to see what Moses was doing in his dust bowl, Moses gave him his cross look. If Mr. Bo Jangles came too close, Moses chased him away. Moses was still learning how to share!

Poor Mr. Bo Jangles—he was quite small compared to Moses. Elephants are the biggest animals in the bush, and while they don't hurt other animals, they do expect all other animals to move out of the way for them.

But at the end of the day, just like quarreling siblings, Mr. Bo Jangles and Moses were still friends.

A Whistling Granny

Moses liked to make human friends too. One day, Granny came to stay. She looked a bit like Mama but with gray hair, and she had lots of time to read stories and play with all the children, even elephant ones. Moses did his favorite activity and used his trunk to explore Granny's face. What a surprise when he got to Granny's ears—she had funny things inside them that Moses tried to take out.

"No, no, Moses, you can't have those. They are Granny's hearing aids and without them in her ears she can't hear anything at all," said Mama. *Okay,* thought Moses. *I won't take them out, but I do still want to feel them with my trunk as they look rather funny.*

But as he moved his trunk close to the hearing aids, they started to whistle— what fun!

A whistling granny! And from that moment on, every time he came close to Granny he moved his trunk up and down near her ears to listen to her hearing aids whistle. It's lucky grannies are so good at being patient with little children—and little elephants.

Moses
Likes
Sharing

M oses was a very friendly little guy and he was very good at sharing (except when it came to Mr. Bo Jangles's dust bowl!). He shared everything . . . even some things that not everybody wanted, like mud.

Elephants love mud. They love to walk in muddy puddles. They love to play in mud. They even like to lie down and roll in mud. Most of all, they like to rub their trunks in mud and then put it all over themselves.

Elephants love mud puddles! It is fun to play in the mud, and it keeps them nice and cool in the hot African sun. Like dust, mud protects elephant skin from sunburn and insects, and it is good for the skin— just ask anyone who goes to expensive spas for mud treatments!

One day, Mama had just finished getting all dressed up to go out—she had a bath, put on a pretty new dress, and did her hair—and popped by to say good-bye to Moses. He was playing with mud at the time and she didn't think about how he loved to share.

Moses looked up at Mama and thought, *Shame, poor Mama looks far too clean to be happy, so I will spread some mud onto her since I know I am always much happier when I am nice and dirty.* So he rubbed his trunk in the squishy brown mud, making sure he got lots and lots of it all over, wandered over to Mama, and rubbed mud all over her face, her hair, and her new dress! Mama was *not* happy! Moses was very confused by Mama's strange reaction.

Surely everybody loves being good and muddy, and Moses really was just trying to share.

Little Catherine Comes Home

It was a very special day at the house. Louise's baby had been born the night before and it was time to bring her home. She was a tiny baby girl called Catherine, and all the family was very excited to meet her. Animals find out about each other by sniffing, as every person and animal has his or her own smell and that is how animals recognize one another. Catherine was going to have a lot of sniffing going on around her! When she came home, all five dogs came to sniff her and say hello, and Moses was not going to be left out. He put his trunk very gently on her head for a good sniff. He then took each little foot one by one into his trunk and held them carefully; it was his way of giving her a cuddle.

But everybody was looking at Catherine and talking to her and Moses felt a little bit ignored. He loved the new baby, but it seemed as if nobody wanted to talk to him anymore. Mama noticed that Moses was standing by himself, sucking on his trunk, which is what baby elephants do if they are a bit sad or unsure, and she went over to give him a cuddle. "We love you lots, Moses. Just because there is a new baby does not mean we love you any less! You will always be our baby and we will always love you." Moses felt much happier and started playing with his ball again.

Sometimes Moses still got a little jealous and caused a bit of a fuss. But even when they are jealous, elephants are always very good at looking after their families. Everyone in the elephant family looks after the babies and gives them lots of love and cuddles with their trunks.

Moses was a very good big brother, and if he ever heard Catherine crying, he ran to go see what was wrong and gently touched her with his trunk, as if to say, *It's all right, Catherine. I am here, and I won't let anything hurt you.*

Good Night,
Moses

When the sun went to bed, Moses had his bottle and went to find Mama to remind her that it was time for them to go to sleep. Moses and Mama slept together on a mattress on the floor. Little elephants can't climb up onto beds and can't be left alone, so Mama had to move onto the mattress. Lucky little Moses!

No bedtime stories for Moses—he was too big to climb onto Mama's knee like little children do. But he could wrap his trunk around Mama's shoulders and ask for a hug, especially when he was a bit sleepy. Moses lay down with Mama and held her hand tightly in his little trunk as he went to sleep.

With such a long nose, he sure snored a lot! Within a few moments he was snoring loudly and dreaming of more adventures.

The End!

Elephant Facts

- A baby elephant is called a calf. An elephant mama is a cow and a daddy is a bull. An elephant family is called a herd.

- Moses drank half a gallon of milk every two hours, daytime and nighttime. He was fed on a unique milk formula made up of forty-five special ingredients and extra nutrients, like casein, whey, lactose, niacin, and calcium. What a lot of milk!

- When little elephants are a bit bigger, they start to eat grass, leaves, and fruit.

- Fully grown elephants weigh as much as a big truck—at least six tons, or 13,200 pounds.

- They grow up to be more than ten feet tall.

- Their trunks grow to be about six feet long and weigh about 176 pounds. That's bigger than the average human!

- Almost all African elephants have tusks, which are very large teeth that can be as heavy as 200 pounds. Elephants start to get tusks at around one year old, and every elephant uses either the left or right tusk more than the other, just as humans are left- or right-handed. Elephants use their tusks to dig up roots to eat, to help dig holes in dry riverbeds to find water, and to protect themselves. Some people like to use tusks as ornaments, but in order to get an elephant's tusks, the elephant has to be killed. This is one reason elephants are targeted by illegal poachers.

- Baby elephants that come to the Jumbo Foundation are eventually reintroduced back into wild elephant families. This is a long process that starts when the baby elephants are about three years old. The babies are slowly introduced to the wild elephants and start to spend longer and longer periods of time with them until one day they decide to move into the new family for good. The keepers stay in the national park with the babies, allowing them to visit with the wild elephants and then come back to the keeper whenever they want to. This process can take many years.

AUTHOR'S NOTE

Moses was a surprise addition to our family, but he inspired all of us and everyone he met. Having him at the Jumbo Foundation taught many people about the importance of preserving and protecting wild elephant habitats. Unfortunately, a short while after this book was written, little Moses got very sick and had to have an operation on his tummy. He had a condition called a herniated umbilical cord. The best elephant doctor in Africa drove all the way from Zambia to Malawi to do the operation on Moses. He did his very best to try and fix Moses, but it was a difficult operation and Moses had to take a lot of antibiotics to help him get better afterward. He was a very brave little elephant and took all his shots without crying, but since the operation was a serious one and there were complications, the problem was just too big for the medicine to fix. One night Moses wrapped his trunk around my hand and went into a very deep, deep sleep, and he did not wake up again. We were all very sad to say good-bye to Moses. But we knew we had to continue the work we'd begun with him. The Jumbo Foundation is now building a special Moses memorial barn for other little elephants and animals that need our help, and we are sure that Moses is looking down at us from elephant heaven and smiling. You are helping us in our mission by taking this time to learn about Moses. If you'd like to learn more about illegal poaching and its effects and what you can do to help orphaned animals, please visit us at JumboFoundation.com.

—Jenny